Polish Wings

Dariusz Karnas

SUKHOI SU-7 & SU-20

Wydawnictwo Stratus s. c. Sandomierz
Skr. poczt. 123, 27-600 Sandomierz 1
tel. +48 (15) 833 30 41
www. stratusbooks.com. pl
office@stratusbooks.com. pl

The author would like to thanks: Bartłomiej Belcarz, Mirosław Czaplicki, Wacław Hołyś, Marek Idzior, Artur Juszczak, Robert Pęczkowski, Paweł Przymusiała, Paweł Sembrat and Mirosław Wasielewski.

Photo credit: Patrick Bigel, Wacław Hołyś, Marek Idzior, Dariusz Karnas, Andrzej Rogucki, Wojciech Sankowski, Paweł Sembrat, Militaria magazine & author's archive.

ISBN 978-83-89450-96-8

Layout concept	Bartłomiej Belcarz
	Artur Bukowski
Cover concept	Artur Juszczak
Cover	Marek Ryś
Translation	Wojtek Matusiak
DTP	Artur Bukowski
	Bartłomiej Belcarz
	Artur Juszczak
Colour Drawings	Artur Juszczak
Proofreading	Roger Wallsgrove

Druk:
Wydawnictwo Diecezjalne i Drukarnia w Sandomierzu
ul. Żeromskiego 4, 27-600 Sandomierz, Poland
phone: +48 15 644 04 00
PRINTED IN POLAND

Media partner in Poland:

AVAILABLE

FORTHCOMING

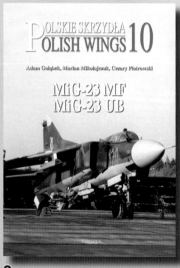
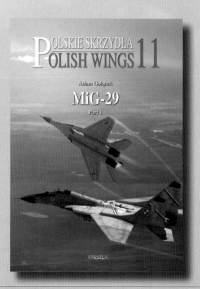
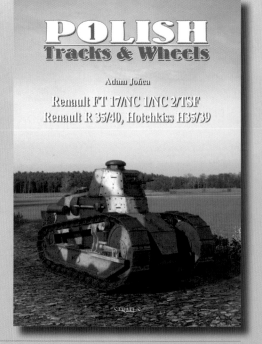

SUKHOI SU-7BM

The late 1950s/early 1960s brought about significant changes in all military services at all levels, from strategic down to tactical. This was due to the rapid proliferation of nuclear weapons, which ceased to be purely strategic. The appearance of tactical nuclear charges cause a true revolution on the battlefield, radically changing the rules of combat, organisation and equipment of the troops. Communist authorities at the time made the assumption that in case of an armed conflict Poland would field two armies, an armoured and a general one, to attack in a north-westerly direction with a single large 'nuclear corridor'. This meant that in the early 1960s Poland needed her own 'nuclear fist'. Needless to say, this would not be an independent force. The Polish Armed Forces were seen as merely an addition and support for the Soviet nuclear forces in the area.

During that time it was decided that in addition to R-170 tactical missiles, Poland should also purchase 36 Su-7 aircraft to form one fighter-bomber aviation regiment. The Su-7s went to the 5th Fighter-Attack Aviation Regiment (5. PLMSz) based in Bydgoszcz, which at the time was part of the 16th Fighter-Attack Aviation Division (16. DLMSz).

Pavel Osipovich Sukhoi started work on a new jet-propelled swept-wing aircraft in 1953, when his design office was reorganised. Previously, while working in the design office of Andrei Tupolev as his deputy, he had prepared designs of two aircraft: S-1 swept-wing front-line fighter and T-3 delta-wing interceptor fighter.

Construction of the first prototype of the S-1 with the AL-7 engine was completed in the summer of 1955. The machine was first flown on 8 September 1955 by A. Ts. Kochetkov. The S-1 was then fitted with the more powerful AL-7F engine giving a thrust of 9,310 daN. In April 1956 V. N. Makhalin flew the S-1 when he established a record for the USSR at 2,170 km/h. Another test pilot, N. I. Korovushkin, used the aircraft to reach an altitude of 19,100 m. The take-off weight of the S-1 was 9,423 kg. Armament consisted of three 30 mm NR-30 cannon. In the autumn of 1957 the aircraft passed state trials, and even before these were completed it was decided to start series production under the military designation Su-7.

The S-1 introduced several innovations to Soviet aircraft. These included the adjustable supersonic air intake and all-moving horizontal tail surfaces. The S-1 was succeeded by the S-2 fighter. Few Su-7s were built as front-line fighters. At the same time Sukhoi was tasked to build a fighter-bomber. It was decided that the new aircraft would be based on the Su-7. The airframe structure was left without significant changes, but new equipment and armament was introduced. The swept wing was retained as the best suited for transition between subsonic and supersonic speeds, without a sharp change of aerodynamic characteristics of the aircraft.

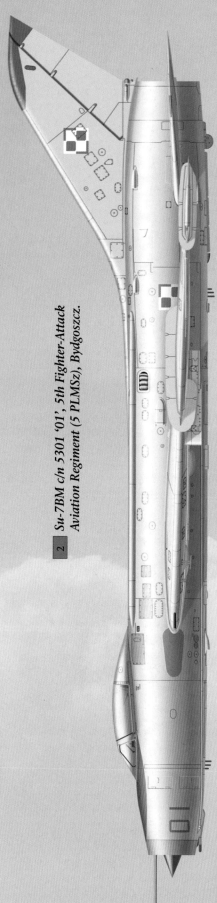

2 *Su-7BM c/n 5301 '01', 5th Fighter-Attack Aviation Regiment (5 PLMSz), Bydgoszcz.*

3

4

[1, 3-5]: *Su-7BM c/n 5301 '01', delivered to the 5th Fighter-Attack Aviation Regiment in Bydgoszcz on 26 June 1964. After 26 years of service, having flown over 1, 100 hours, on 29 August 1990 it was transferred to the Aircraft Depot at Mierzęcice. In October 1990 the aircraft was handed over to the Polish Aviation Museum in Cracow.*

5

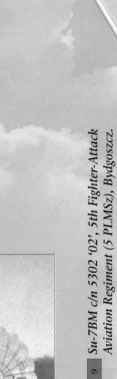

Su-7BM c/n 5302 '02', 5th Fighter-Attack Aviation Regiment (5 PLMSz), Bydgoszcz.

[6-8]: *Su-7BM c/n 5302 '02', on 26 June 1964 delivered to the 5th Fighter-Attack Aviation Regiment in Bydgoszcz.*

C/N	CODE NO.	PRODUCTION DATE / DELIVERY DATE	UNIT	NOTES
5301	01	31. 05. 1964/26. 06. 1964	5 PLMSz	Struck off charge on 29 August 1990. Currently at the MLP in Cracow.
5302	02	31. 05. 1964/26. 06. 1964	5 PLMSz	Struck off charge on 29 August 1990 and scrapped[1].
5303	03	31. 05. 1964/26. 06. 1964	5 PLMSz	Struck off charge on 1 March 1991 and transferred to the WZL-2 in Bydgoszcz. Currently on display at the 2nd Air Base (2 BL) in Bydgoszcz with a fictitious code no. '3117'.
5305	05	31. 05. 1964/26. 06. 1964	5 PLMSz	Destroyed in a crash on 11 November 1970.
5306	06	31. 05. 1964/26. 06. 1964	5 PLMSz	Struck off charge on 18 December 1989. Currently at the MLP in Cracow.
5309	09	31. 05. 1964/26. 06. 1964	5 PLMSz	Struck off charge on 7 August 1980 and transferred to the COSSTWL at Oleśnica.

In April 1959 E. Solovyev made the first flight in the prototype of the new fighter-bomber designated the S-22. The official report from the state trials said that the specifications and armament of the S-22 far exceeded all other aircraft of similar role.

When introduced into series production, the S-22 was given the military designation Su-7B (and the NATO reporting name 'Fitter-A'). The Su-7B was a supersonic fighter-bomber and reconnaissance aircraft.

The Sukhoi Su-7 was subject to continuous changes and modifications. The next production version was designated the Su-7BM (S-22M; M for modifitsirovanniy). The Su-7BM had a slightly altered fuselage and modified avionics. The pitot was repositioned to starboard of the centreline. The brake parachute container was fitted under the fuselage.

The first six Polish Su-7BMs were delivered to the 1st Flight of the 5th Fighter-Attack Aviation Regiment on 26 June 1964. The aircraft were from the 53rd production batch. Two-digit numbers were applied on sides of the machines, these being the endings of their factory numbers: '01', '02', '03', '05', '06', '09'. The numbers were applied in red. The aircraft delivered to the 1st Flight were the only examples of the BM version used by the Polish Air Force.

Polish pilots who were going to fly the Su-7s were trained at the Higher Aviation-Technical Officers' School at Krasnodar in the USSR. Experienced officers, with at least 600-700 hours flown in Lim fighters (MiGs licence-built in Poland) were selected. Training on the new type was unusual in that the Russians, who did not have Su-7U two-seaters, used the two-seat MiG-21U for the purpose. The lighter and significantly more manoeuvrable MiG-21 differed a lot from the Su-7 in terms of flying characteristics, and Polish pilots could only make one flight in it before they moved to the single-seat Su-7s. The quality of the of Polish pilots is best proved by the fact that they suffered no accidents during training in the USSR.

Polish Air Force Su-7s were first shown to the Polish public during a parade on 22 July 1966 to celebrate 1,000 years of Poland.

[10]: Su-7BM c/n 5301 '01', during engine start-up at the 5th Fighter-Attack Aviation Regiment base in Bydgoszcz.

The following year brought organisation changes to the Bydgoszcz-based unit. On 4 May 1967 the 5th Fighter-Bomber Aviation Regiment (5 PLMB) was renumbered the 3rd 'Pomorski' Fighter-Bomber Aviation Regiment (3 PLMB).

The first Su-7BM lost in Polish service was code no. 05. The accident took place on 11 November 1970 during training at the Solec Kujawski firing range. The aircraft was lost when its engine stalled after firing S-24 unguided missiles. The pilot, mjr Izydor Olszewski, ejected safely.

On 29 August 1975 an Su-7BM, code no. '09', flown by kpt. Stanisław Wróblewski, suffered a burst tyre during landing at Piła. As a consequence the aircraft swung off the runway and was seriously damaged. Its repair proved uneconomical and the ill-fated '09' was transferred as a ground instructional airframe to the Polish Air Force Central Training Establishment of Technical Specialists (COSSTWL) at Oleśnica.

[11-12]: Su-7BM c/n 5306 '06', now on display at the Polish Aviation Museum in Cracow.

Polish Wings

[13]: Su-7BM c/n 5303 '03'. Struck off charge on 1 March 1991 and transferred to the Military Aircraft Works 2 (WZL-2) in Bydgoszcz. Currently on display at the 2nd Air Base in Bydgoszcz with a fictitious code no. '3117'.

[14]: Su-7BM c/n 5306 '06'. 600 l drop tanks can be seen under the fuselage.

[15]: Su-7BM c/n 5309 '09'. In August 1975 the aircraft flown by kpt. Stanisław Wróblewski suffered a burst tyre during landing at Piła and swung off the runway. The aircraft proved damaged beyond economical repair. Struck off charge on 7 August 1980, it was transferred as a ground instructional airframe to the Polish Air Force Central Training Establishment of Technical Specialists at Oleśnica. Now it is in an aviation museum in Germany.

16 *Su-7BM c/n 5303 '03', 5th Fighter-Attack Aviation Regiment (5 PLMSz), Bydgoszcz.*

17 *Su-7BM c/n 5306 '06', 5th Fighter-Attack Aviation Regiment (5 PLMSz), Bydgoszcz.*

18 *Su-7BM c/n 5309 '09', 5th Fighter-Attack Aviation Regiment (5 PLMSz), Bydgoszcz.*

SUKHOI SU-7BKL

The next version, designated the Su-7BKL (S-22KL; KL for 'koleso-lizhniy' or 'wheel-ski'), was fitted with additional skis on the undercarriage. This allowed the machines to operate from unprepared airfields. During take-off and landing on such landing grounds, as the wheels sank into the ground the aircraft was supported by the skis.

As a result of critical remarks by pilots regarding the too long landing run of the aircraft, two ribbon brake parachutes were fitted in a fairing at the base of the fin. The Su-7BKL was powered by the AL-7 F-1-200 engine. The Su-7BMK was the next development version, which had, among other changes, an increased payload thanks to its strengthened structure.

New Su-7s, the BKL version, arrived in Bydgoszcz on 7 July 1966. These were 12 new machines from the 60th production batch. They had code numbers from 12 to 23 (serials 6012-6023).

3 PLMB lost its first aircraft on 9 October 1967 when the Su-7BKL code no. '21' suffered a leak in the engine lubrica-

tion system, which led to engine seizure. The pilot, por. Ryszard Zaperty, ejected safely.

Two more Su-7BKLs were delivered to the 3 PLMB on 29 January 1968. The machines came from the 65th production batch. To avoid repeating code numbers used on the earlier aircraft, three-digit codes were introduced, these matching the ending of the construction number. These aircraft were coded '515' and '516'. These Su-7BKLs were originally built for an Arab country, as shown by stencils in English in the cockpit. These aircraft also featured a somewhat different

19

20

21

25 *Su-7BKL c/n 7926 '926', 3rd Fighter-Bomber Aviation Regiment (3 PLMB), Bydgoszcz.*

[19-24]: Su-7BKL c/n 7926 '926', delivered on 12 May 1972 to the 3rd Fighter-Bomber Aviation Regiment in Bydgoszcz. UB-16 pods for 57 mm S-5 unguided missiles can be seen on outer under-wing hardpoints. On 29 August 1990 the aircraft, having logged a total of 1, 720 flying hours, was delivered to the Aircraft Depot at Mierzęcice, and thence to the airfield of the Opole Flying Club.

[29]: Su-7BKL c/n 6014 '14', 5th Fighter-Bomber Aviation Regiment (5 PLMB), Bydgoszcz.

[26]: *Su-7BKL c/n 6014 '14', on 7 July 1966 to the 5th Fighter-Bomber Aviation Regiment in Bydgoszcz. The aircraft has 600 l fuel tanks on inboard under-wing hardpoints, and UB-16 pods for 57 mm S-5 unguided missiles on outboard under-wing hardpoints.*

[27]: *The aircraft in the photos has 600 l fuel tanks on under-fuselage hardpoints and UB-16 pods on outboard under-wing hardpoints.*

[28]: *One of the differences between the Su-7BKL and the BM version was the fairing for two ribbon brake parachutes at the base of the fin.*

[30-32]: Su-7BKL c/n 6015 '15', delivered on 7 July 1966 to the 5th Fighter-Bomber Aviation Regiment in Bydgoszcz. UB-16 pods for 57 mm S-5 unguided missiles can be seen on outer under-wing hardpoints, and 600 l fuel tanks on under-fuselage hardpoints. The aircraft was lost on 18 July 1984, kpt. Wiktor Korczyński ejecting safely. The accident was due to engine failure.

Su-7BKL c/n 6015 '15', 5th Fighter-Bomber Aviation Regiment (5 PLMB), Bydgoszcz.

34 *Su-7BKL c/n 6021 '21', 5th Fighter-Bomber Aviation Regiment (5 PLMB), Bydgoszcz.*

[35]: Su-7BKL c/n 6023 '23', delivered on 7 July 1966 to the 5th Fighter-Bomber Aviation Regiment in Bydgoszcz. In February 1971 the aircraft was delivered to Czechoslovakia to replace a Czechoslovak machine shot down the previous July by a Polish pilot, kpt. Henryk Osierda.

[36, 37]: Su-7BKL c/n 6021 '21' delivered on 7 July 1966 to the 5th Fighter-Bomber Aviation Regiment in Bydgoszcz. No. '21' was the first aircraft of the type lost by the Polish Air Force. The aircraft suffered a leak in the engine lubrication system, which led to engine seizure. The pilot, por. Ryszard Zaperty ejected safely. The accident took place on 9 October 1967.

[38]: *APU-14 pods for seven S-3K unguided missiles can be seen on under-fuselage and outboard under-wing hardpoints.*

[39, 40]: *Su-7BKL c/n 7808 '808', delivered to the 3rd Fighter-Bomber Aviation Regiment in Bydgoszcz in September 1971. On 29 August 1990, having logged a total of 2, 100 flying hours, the aircraft went to the Aircraft Depot at Mierzęcice where it was scrapped. UB-16 pods for 57 mm S-5 unguided missiles can be seen on under-wing and under-fuselage hardpoints.*

41 *Su-7BKL c/n 7808 '808', 3rd Fighter-Bomber Aviation Regiment (3 PLMB), Bydgoszcz.*

[42, 43]: FAB-250M46 HE bomb.

[44, 45]: Engine inlet duct and outlet nozzle protective plugs.

[46, 47]: Attaching the FAB-250M46 HE bomb under the aircraft fuselage.

[48, 49]: Attaching the FAB-250M46 HE bomb and S-5 unguided missiles in the UB-16-57U pod under the aircraft fuselage.

C/N	CODE NO.	PRODUCTION DATE / DELIVERY DATE	UNIT	NOTES
6012	12	31.03.1966 / 07.07.1966	5 PLMB	Struck off charge on 18 July 1990. Currently on display at a private collection in Łódź.
6013	13	31.03.1966 / 07.07.1966	5 PLMB	Struck off charge on 17 July 1990. Currently at the MWP in Warsaw.
0614	14	31.03.1966 / 07.07.1966	5 PLMB	Struck off charge on 16 July 1990 and scrapped.
6015	15	31.03.1966 / 07.07.1966	5 PLMB	Destroyed on 18 July 1984.
6016	16	31.03.1966 / 07.07.1966	5 PLMB	Struck off charge on 30 August 1990 and scrapped.
6017	17	31.03.1966 / 07.07.1966	5 PLMB	Struck off charge on 17 July 1990. Currently at the MWP in Warsaw.
6018	18	31.03.1966 / 07.07.1966	5 PLMB	Struck off charge on 30 August 1990 and scrapped.
6019	19	31.03.1966 / 07.07.1966	5 PLMB	Struck off charge on 16 July 1990 and scrapped.
6020	20	31.03.1966 / 07.07.1966	5 PLMB	Struck off charge on 17 July 1990 and scrapped.
6021	21	31.03.1966 / 07.07.1966	5 PLMB	Destroyed on 9 October 1967.
6022	22	31.03.1966 / 07.07.1966	5 PLMB	Struck off charge on 30 August 1990. Currently on display at a private collection in Łódź.
6023	23	31.03.1966 / 07.07.1966	5 PLMB	On 26 February 1971 handed over to the Czechoslovak Air Force.
6515	515	10.1967 / 29.01.1968	3 PLMB	Destroyed on 12 June 1987.
6516	516	10.1967 / 29.01.1968	3 PLMB	Struck off charge on 16 July 1990 and scrapped.
7806	806	06.1971 / 07.09.1971	3 PLMB	Struck off charge on 18 December 1989 and transferred to the MLP in Cracow.
7807	807	06.1971 / 07.09.1971	3 PLMB	Struck off charge on 18 July 1990 and transferred to the MLP in Cracow.
7808	808	06.1971 / 07.09.1971	3 PLMB	Struck off charge on 29 August 1990 and scrapped.
7809	809	06.1971 / 07.09.1971	3 PLMB	Struck off charge on 29 August 1990 and transferred to the 'White Eagle' Museum at Skarżysko-Kamienna.
7810	810	08.1971 / 11.04.1972	3 PLMB	Destroyed on 24 November 1982.
7812	812	08.1971 / 11.04.1972	3 PLMB	Struck off charge on 16 July 1990 and scrapped.
7813	813	08.1971 / 11.04.1972	3 PLMB	Struck off charge on 18 July 1990 and scrapped.
7815	815	08.1971 / 11.04.1972	3 PLMB	Struck off charge 30 August 1990. Currently at the MWP in Warsaw.
7816	816	08.1971 / 11.04.1972	3 PLMB	Struck off charge on 21 September 1990 and scrapped.
7818	818	09.1971 / 11.04.1972	3 PLMB	Struck off charge on 17 July 1990 and scrapped.
7819	819	09.1971 / 11.04.1972	3 PLMB	Struck off charge on 29 August 1990 and scrapped.
7820	820	09.1971 / 11.04.1972	3 PLMB	Destroyed on 1 August 1984.
7821	821	09.1971 / 11.04.1972	3 PLMB	Struck off charge on 17 July 1990 and scrapped.
7910	910	08.1971 / 11.04.1972	3 PLMB	Destroyed on 21 June 1972.
7911	911	12.1971 / 11.04.1972	3 PLMB	Struck off charge on 29 August 1990 and scrapped.
7926	926	04.1972 / 11.04.1972	3 PLMB	Struck off charge on 29 August 1990 and scrapped.
8004	804	16.05.1972 / 15.01.1988	3 PLMB	Struck off charge on 16 July 1990 and scrapped.

adjustment of the control column artificial loading. This fact led to a different take-off technique, as the machines showed a tendency to raise the nose by themselves. Pilots who flew them called them 'Arabs', and they were not well liked.

In February 1971 one Su-7BKL (6023/23) was struck off charge and delivered to Czechoslovakia in exchange for a Czechoslovak machine shot down by accident the previous July during the international military exercise 'Zenit 70'. On 14 July 1970 a Czechoslovak Su-7BKL was intercepted by a pair of Polish MiG-21PFMs of the 11th Fighter Aviation Regiment (11 PLM) based in Wrocław. One of their pilots, kpt. Henryk Osierda, had to change aircraft immediately prior to take-off. In the heat of the exercise, due to lack of another flight-ready MiG, the pilot was ordered to take off in a QRA aircraft. The MiG-21 was armed with two live R-3S ('Atoll-A') missiles. The pilot of the interceptor forgot the crucial fact that instead of training pods his aircraft carried live weapons and fired a well-aimed missile into the Czech Su-7. The Czechoslovak pilot ejected safely from his aircraft.

More Su-7 aircraft were delivered to the 3 PLMB on 7 September 1971. The four new machines, Su-7BKLs, bore code nos. '806', '807', '808', '809' and were from the 78th production batch.

In 1972 the last twelve Su-7BKLs were delivered to Bydgoszcz. On 11 April nine machines from the 78th production batch were delivered. They bore code numbers: '810'; '812'; '813'; '815'; '816'; '818'; '819'; '820'; '821'. Two more aircraft, code numbers '910' and '911', were from the 79th production batch. On 24 May 1972 the last of the 36 combat aircraft on order reached Bydgoszcz. It was from the 79th production batch and had code no. '926'.

A month later the machine code no. '910' was destroyed in a crash. This took place on 26 June 1972, and the pilot, por. Albinat Tomaszewski, was killed.

After that crash the 3 PLMB had 32 Su-7 fighter-bombers, including 5 Su-7BMs and 27 Su-7BKLs. The unit also had three Su-7U combat trainers. This establishment of the regiment was maintained for the next ten years.

[50]

[50]: *Su-7BKL c/n 6515 '515', delivered to the 3rd Fighter-Bomber Aviation Regiment in Bydgoszcz in January 1968. The aircraft was written off by a Russian pilot in a crash at Biała Podlaska on 12 June 1987.*

[51]

[52]

[51, 52]: *Su-7BKL c/n 7820 '820 ', delivered to the 3rd Fighter-Bomber Aviation Regiment in Bydgoszcz on 11 April 1972. It crashed on 1 August 1984 at Nadarzyce firing range. During firing of S-5 unguided missiles against ground targets mjr Zdzisław Fendrych recovered the machine too violently from a dive, causing it to flip onto its back and then spin. The aircraft hit ground at a speed of approx. 470 km/h, killing the pilot.*

[53]

[53]: *Su-7BKL c/n 7812 ' 812 ', delivered to the 3rd Fighter-Bomber Aviation Regiment in Bydgoszcz on 11 April 1972. On 16 July 1990 the aircraft, having logged a total of 1, 860 flying hours, was delivered to the Aircraft Depot at Mierzęcice, and then sold.*

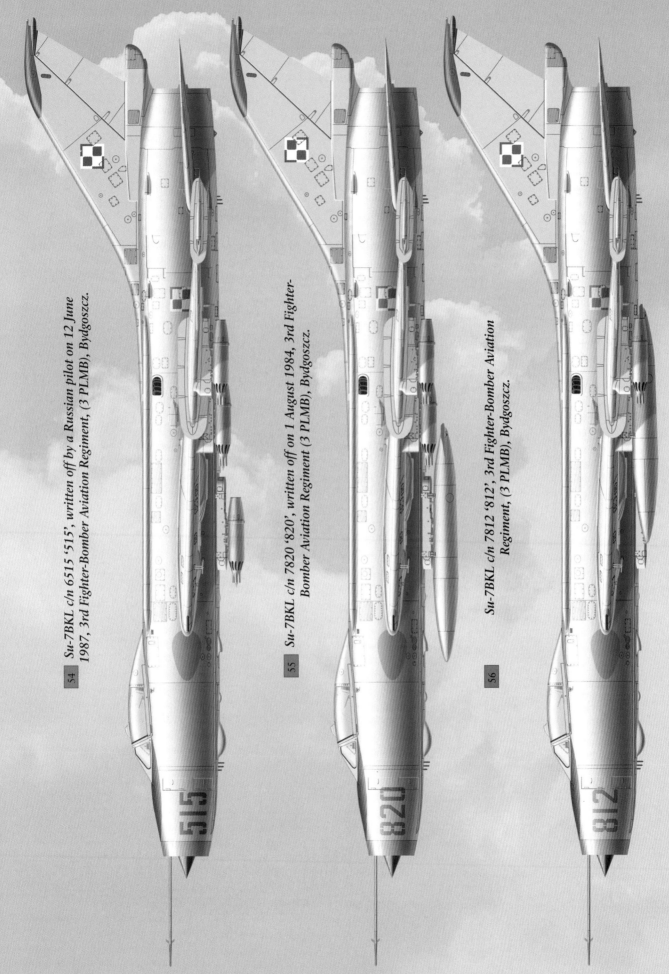

54   *Su-7BKL c/n 6515 '515', written off by a Russian pilot on 12 June 1987, 3rd Fighter-Bomber Aviation Regiment, (3 PLMB), Bydgoszcz.*

55   *Su-7BKL c/n 7820 '820', written off on 1 August 1984, 3rd Fighter-Bomber Aviation Regiment (3 PLMB), Bydgoszcz.*

56   *Su-7BKL c/n 7812 '812', 3rd Fighter-Bomber Aviation Regiment, (3 PLMB), Bydgoszcz.*

[57]: *A rare photo to bring back the times of communist propaganda. Su-7BKL c/n 7911 '911' delivered to 3 PLMB in Bydgoszcz on 11 April 1972 with Edward Gierek (the head of the communist party in Poland), Henryk Jabłoński (the President of the State Council) and Wojciech Jaruzelski (the Minister of Defence).*

57

The early 1980s brought a number of dangerous accidents, two of which ended tragically. On 24 November 1982 the Su-7BKL code no. '810' was lost and por. Marek Gawłowski was killed. Another Su-7BKL was lost on 18 July 1984, when kpt. Wiktor Korczyński ejected safely from the machine code no. '15'.

On 12 June 1987 the Su-7BKL code no. '515' was lost in unusual circumstances. A Russian pilot who ferried the aircraft to the USSR for an overhaul, but who had not flown the Su-7 for a long time, forgot the type's well known excessive fuel consumption. Having used afterburner several times at low level near Biała Podlaska, he realised he faced a fuel crisis. After unsuccessful attempts to establish communication with the air base at Biała Podlaska he was forced to eject. The unfortunate pilot suffered a serious financial loss, as he had done quite substantial shopping in Poland. The Soviets admitted the fault of their own pilot and on 15 January 1988 replaced the loss with an aircraft from the 80th production batch, no. 8004. The aircraft had been built in 1972 and used extensively for over fifteen years in the Soviet Air Force. In the Polish Air Force it was given the code no. '804'. The changes and upgrades that this aircraft had undergone in Soviet service led to a joke among the 3 PLMB technical personnel, that the unit operated four versions of the Su-7: the Su-7U, Su-7BM, Su-7BKL and '804'.

Su-7s flew their last flights in the Polish Air Force during the summer of 1990. At that time 27 Su-7s (2 Su-7BMs, 21 Su-7BKLs and 4 Su-7Us) were transferred to the depot at Mierzęcice, where they were scrapped. The remaining machines went, among others, to the Polish Aviation Museum in Cracow, Polish Army Museum in Warsaw (Czerniakowski Fort), 'White Eagle' Museum at Skarżysko-Kamienna and a private collection at Hermeskeil (Germany).

[58]: *Su-7BKLs on a forward aerodrome during an exercise in 1977. Aircraft '818', '806', '13' and '808' covered by masking nets.*

58

SUKHOI SU-7U

The Su-7 was the basis for a two-seat combat trainer version used for operational training and for pilot conversion training. The machine was designated the Su-7U (U-22). Subsequent development versions were designated the Su-7UM (U-22M) and Su-7UMK (U-22MK). They were known in the NATO code as the 'Moujik'.

On 25 September 1969 the first two Su-7U combat trainers arrived in Bydgoszcz. The machines were from the 21st production batch and bore code numbers '115' and '116'.

In September 1971 an Su-7U, construction number 3313, was delivered to Bydgoszcz. To avoid the 'unlucky thirteen', the aircraft was given the code no. '331', i. e. the first rather than the last three digits of the construction number.

In late 1970s Poland took delivery of more Su-7U aircraft. This was connected with the conversion of the 7th Operational Reconnaissance Aviation Brigade at Powidz from the Il-28 ('Beagle') onto the Su-20 commenced in 1974. Because there was no two-seater version of the Su-20, it was decided to use the Su-7U as the training machine. The first Su-7U, c/n 3513, was delivered on 7 July 1976. This time nobody was afraid of the 'unlucky thirteen' and the last three digits of the construction number were applied on

the side as code no. '513'. However, the aircraft was lost in a crash in 1981.

C/n 3513 was joined at Powidz at about the same time by another Su-7U, c/n 3702. The machine received the code no. '702' and was approximately as old as its predecessor. The third Su-7U, c/n 3517 (code no. '517') was delivered to the 7th Bomber-Reconnaissance Aviation Brigade at Powidz on 12 February 1977.

On 25 March 1977 an Su-7U was delivered to the 3 PLMB in Bydgoszcz. This was the fourth of the 'U' version machines purchased at the time. The last Su-7U was delivered to Powidz on 16 June 1984. It is intriguing that the machine had been built fourteen years earlier!

The Su-7U aircraft used at Powidz were transferred to the 3 PLMB in Bydgoszcz during March-August 1986. The 7th Bomber-Reconnaissance Aviation Regiment took delivery of its first Su-22UM3K aircraft at the time.

On 23 April 1985 the 3 PLMB in Bydgoszcz lost its Su-7U code no. '115'. The accident took place during a practice sortie dropping a B-50 bomb in upward flight (the so-called 'toss bombing'). During the flight the external fuel tanks were accidentally jettisoned and damaged the elevators. The pilots, por. Struj and mjr Czerwiński ejected safely.

[59]: *The first Su-7U combat trainers were delivered to the 3rd Fighter-Bomber Aviation Regiment in Bydgoszcz on 25 September 1969. They were 21st production batch machines and were given code numbers '115' (c/n 2115) and '116' (c/n 2116). This photo shows the Su-7U c/n 3706 '706', delivered to the 3 PLMB in Bydgoszcz on 25 March 1977 and the Su-7BKL c/n 6016 '6016', delivered to the 5th Fighter-Bomber Aviation Regiment in Bydgoszcz on 7 July 1966. An FAB-250M46 bomb is carried on the trolley towed by the tractor.*

59

C/N	CODE NO.	PRODUCTION DATE / DELIVERY DATE	UNIT	NOTES
2115	115	06.1969 / 25.09.1969	3 PLMB	Destroyed on 23 April 1985.
2116	116	07.1969 / 25.09.1969	3 PLMB	Also used for a while by the 7 BLRO. Struck off charge on 29 November 1989 and transferred to the MLP in Cracow.
3313	331	04.1971 / 07.09.1971	3 PLMB, 7 PLBR	Struck off charge on 18 July 1990 and transferred to the MWP in Warsaw.
3513	513	18.08.1971 / 07.07. 1976	3 PLMB, 7 PLBR	Destroyed on 16 March 1982.
3702	702	23.12.1971 / 07.07.1976	7 BLRO, 3 PLMB, 7 PLBR	Struck off charge on 29 August 1990. Currently on display at a private collection in Łódź.
3517	517	28.11.1971 / 12.02.1977	3 PLMB, 7 PLBR	Struck off charge on 16 July 1990 and scrapped.
3706	706	28.01.1972 / 25.03.1977	3 PLMB, 7 PLBR	Struck off charge on 29 August 1990 and scrapped.
2905	905	18.08.1970 / 16.06.1984	7 PLBR, 3 PLMB	On 24 March 1986 transferred to the 3 PLMB. Struck off charge on 17 November 1989 and transferred to the Museum at Drzonów.

[60]: *Su-7U c/n 2905 ' 905', delivered to the 7th Bomber-Reconnaissance Aviation Regiment at Powidz on 16 June 1984.*

[61, 62]: *Delivery of the two-seat Su-7 version to Powidz was connected with the conversion of the 7th Operational Reconnaissance Aviation Brigade at Powidz from the Il-28 ('Beagle') onto the Su-20 commenced in 1974. Because there was no two-seater version of the Su-20, it was decided to use the Su-7U as the training machine. '905' was transferred to the 3rd Fighter-Bomber Aviation Regiment in Bydgoszcz in March 1986. Currently on display at the Lubuskie Military Museum at Drzonów.*

[66] Su-7U c/n 3313 '331', written off on 18 July 1984, 3rd Fighter-Bomber Aviation Regiment (3PLMB), Bydgoszcz.

[63-65]: Su-7U c/n 3313 '331', delivered to the 3 PLMB in Bydgoszcz in September 1971. To avoid the 'unlucky thirteen', the aircraft was given the code no. '331'. The Su-7U '702' (c/n 3702) delivered to 3 PLMB in Bydgoszcz in July 1976 can be seen in the background. The aircraft was used for several years by the 7 BLBR at Powidz. Currently on display at a Polish Military Museum in Warsaw..

[67]: *Su-7U c/n 2115 '115', delivered to 3 PLMB in Bydgoszcz in September 1969. The aircraft was destroyed on 23 April 1985 during a practice sortie. During the flight external fuel tanks were accidentally jettisoned and damaged the elevators. The pilots, por. Struj and mjr Czerwiński, ejected safely.*

[68]: *Su-7U c/n 2116 '116', in September 1969 was first delivered to the 3 PLMB in Bydgoszcz. The machine was transferred to Powidz for a short time, and then it returned to Bydgoszcz. On 29 November 1989 the aircraft was struck off charge and transferred to the Polish Aviation Museum (MLP) in Cracow.*

[69]: *Su-7U c/n 3706 '706', delivered to 3 PLMB in Bydgoszcz on 25 March 1977. After thirteen years of operation it was struck off charge in July 1990 and scrapped.*

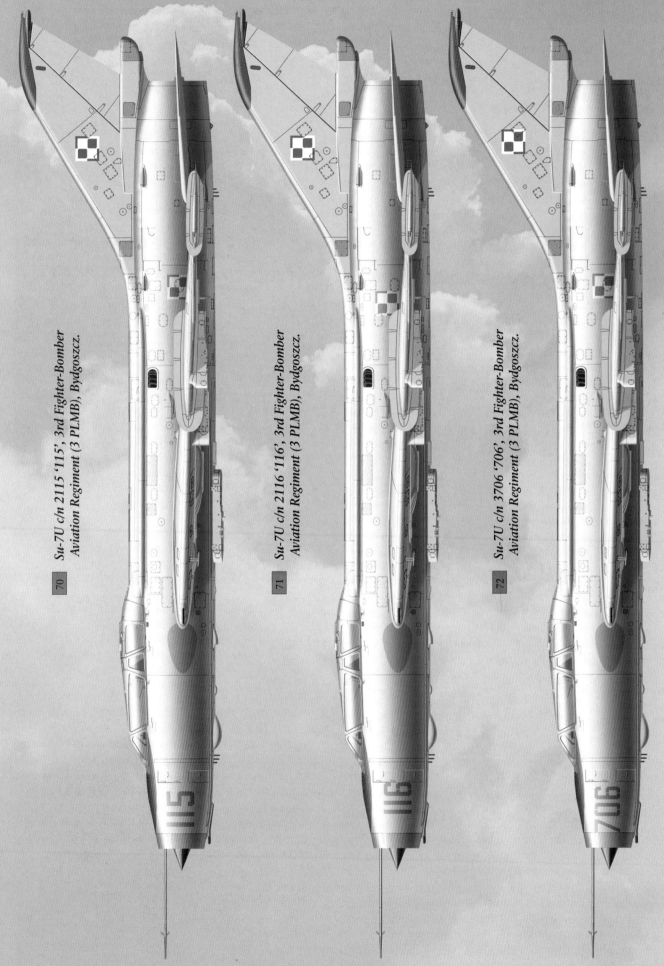

70 *Su-7U c/n 2115 '115', 3rd Fighter-Bomber Aviation Regiment (3 PLMB), Bydgoszcz.*

71 *Su-7U c/n 2116 '116', 3rd Fighter-Bomber Aviation Regiment (3 PLMB), Bydgoszcz.*

72 *Su-7U c/n 3706 '706', 3rd Fighter-Bomber Aviation Regiment (3 PLMB), Bydgoszcz.*

[73]: Su-7U c/n 3706 awaits take-off clearance.

[74]: Su-7U c/n 3706 '3706', ppor. Krzyszytof Przybylski prepares for a flight with instructor mjr Edward Peczka.

COLOURS OF SUKHOI 7

Aircraft delivered from the USSR were initially in natural duralumin finish overall, with the exception of the steel panels near the wing-mounted cannon ports. The only outstanding colour components were the green (FS 34227/34128) aerial fairings at the top of the fin and engine air intake cones. Some aircraft had red code numbers applied using stencils used in the Soviet Air Force.

Upon acceptance of the machines by Polish units the aircraft had Polish national markings applied with stencils on both sides of the fuselage and fin, and on wing under surfaces.

On aircraft that did not have their code numbers on delivery these were applied at their destination airfields. Since initially there were no standardised stencils, code numbers were applied using stencils used earlier on MiG-15 and Lim-2 aircraft.

Aircraft that were subsequently overhauled were painted silver (FS 17178) overall. Top of fuselage ahead of the windscreen was painted blue-grey (FS 35526), intended as an antiglare panel. A 630 mm band of the same colour was applied on each wing root along the fuselage.

Overhauls of worn machines led to a change of code number shapes. The stencils were mostly standardised. The numbers were applied with gloss red paint (FS 11400) some 500 mm from the engine air intake. The style of code number digits was similar to that used on MiG-21s.

Servicing stencils in Russian were applied in blue (FS 35052) on the entire airframe, with the exception of red (FS 31302) stencils on the main under-fuselage weapon carriers.

Cockpit interior was blue-grey (FS 35550/35526), sometimes repainted grey during overhauls, with the exception of the black instrument panel.

Main and nose wheel wells were originally painted blue-grey (FS 24233). Subsequently they were repeatedly repainted with paints currently used for overhauls in the units (FS 24432, FS 26187, for example). Wheel legs were blue-grey (FS 35526/35550). Wheel discs were originally green (FS 24227), but were then periodically repainted (34108, for example).

Under-wing radio-altimeter aerials, originally green (FS 34108), were repainted blue-green (FS 34058).

[75]: *Aircraft delivered from the USSR were initially in natural duralumin finish overall, with exception of the steel panels near the wing-mounted cannon ports. The only outstanding colour components were the green (FS 34227/34128) aerial fairings at the top of the fin and engine air intake cones. Aircraft that were subsequently overhauled were painted silver colour (FS 17178) overall. Top of fuselage ahead of the windscreen was painted blue-grey (FS 35526) intended as an anti-glare panel. A 630 mm band of the same colour was applied on each wing root along the fuselage.*

SUKHOI SU-20

In parallel with the start of series production of the Su-7, development of the aircraft continued. Particular stress was placed on developing a variable geometry (swing wing) combat aircraft.

It was decided to use the Su-7 as the basis, and unlike other swing wing aircraft developed at the time (such as the MiG-23), only the outer wing panels were moving in the Sukhoi machine. A broad aerodynamic fence, some 4 m long, was fitted on the outer edge of the fixed wing centre section to strengthen the structure, allowing carriage of armament or fuel tanks there. The fixed wing centre section was thickened. By retaining a large non-moving portion of the wing it was easier to arrange the undercarriage and external armament stores. Shift of the aerodynamic centre while swinging the wing was small and generally balanced by the shift in centre of gravity. Moving wing panels were fitted with leading and trailing edge flaps which, coupled with the wing sweep change, significantly improved take-off and landing characteristics.

The experimental aircraft was designated the Su-7IG (IG for 'izmenayemaya geometriya' or 'variable geometry').

The Su-7IG (known as the 'Fitter-B' to NATO), was an experimental aircraft used for in-depth research of the variable geometry wing. Series production of the aircraft developed from it was soon begun. The aircraft bore the designation Su-17 (S-32). Series production of the aircraft was undertaken from 1970 at Komsomolsk-on-Amur.

In 1972 the Su-17 was replaced by the Su-17M, the latter's export version being known as the Su-20, 'Fitter C' in the NATO code. The main change was the new AL-21F3 engine which produced greater thrust but was lighter. This allowed an increase in payload from 3, 000 kg to 4, 000 kg. Equipment included the ASP-PFM-7 gun sight and the PBK-2 bomb sight. The aircraft had two built-in NR-30 cannon in the wing roots. External armament included Kh-23M ('Kerry') guided missiles, unguided missiles, conventional and nuclear bombs. From 1974 the aircraft was also able to carry the Kh-25 ('Karen') and Kh-29 ('Kedge') missiles thanks to using an external target illuminating pod.

Su-17 (Su-20) DEVELOPMENT VERSIONS
- Su-17 - intermediate production version (1970-1973) that differed from the prototype with a redesigned nose. This was a single-seat attack-bomber. Powered by Saturn/Lulka AL-21F3 engine (6, 670/9, 420 daN), several initial examples had the AL-7F1 engine. Armament was carried on eight hardpoints under the fuselage and the fixed wing section.
- Su-17M - ultimate version (1973-1975) with the AL-21F3 engine (7, 650/10, 990 daN). Increased fuel tankage, external tanks 2 x 1, 150 l, 2 x 800 l, Kh-23 guided missiles (with Delta-NG) and R-3S/R-13M AAMs. Differed from the Su-17 in having additional fences on top of the wing.
- Su-17R - reconnaissance variant of the Su-17M.
- Su-17M2 and Su-17M2D - modified Su-17M with longer nose inclined downwards for improved forward visibility. This was the first version with Doppler radar and laser range finder in the cone.
- Su-20 - export version of the Su-17M. Used by the Polish Air Force, among others.
- Su-20U - export version of the Su-17UM.
- Su-20R - export version of the Su-17R.

[76]: *Su-20 aircraft at Powidz airfield. Comparison of each of the Su-20 shows that there are differences in camouflage details, but colours and overall patterns are almost the same.*

76

[77]: *Four 800 l fuel tanks can be seen on under-wing and under-fuselage hardpoints. The aircraft made its last flight on 28 February 1997, when kpt. Andrzej Paczkowski ferried it to the repair works in Bydgoszcz. The aircraft logged a total flying time of 1, 392 hrs 3 mins.*

In 1973 Polish civil and military authorities decided to procure a successor for the Il-28 then leaving service. To meet the expectations of the Poles, the Soviets offered MiG-23B or Su-20 aircraft. Despite doubts voiced by the committee that defined specifications for the new aircraft, and against a clearly negative opinion in the final phase, it was decided to purchase the Su-20. Political reality of that time was such that no expert opinions were taken into consideration, and certainly no economic factors were considered important.

In early 1974 the first group of pilots and technicians went to Krasnodar in the USSR to undergo theoretical and practical training on the new type. Another group of flying and ground personnel underwent training in the USSR in 1975.

The first Su-20s arrived at Powidz on 26 April 1974. They were six machines of the 66th production batch (S-32MK). They had consecutive construction numbers 6601 to 6606, and code numbers '01' to '06'. In 1975 two-digit numbers on Su-20s were replaced with four-digit ones of '4241' to '4246'.

Su-20s were first shown to general public during a flypast on 22 July 1974 over Warsaw.

In 1976 the principal delivery took place, when twenty Su-20s arrived. This led to another change of the unit name. By the orders of the Commander of the Air Force no. PF167 of 27 July 1976 the 7th Operational Reconnaissance Aviation Brigade (7 BLRO) was renamed the 7th Bomber-Reconnaissance

Aviation Brigade (BLBR). Aircraft delivered at the time were given four-digit code numbers. Each digit of the number had a distinct meaning. The first digit was the last digit of the year the aircraft was delivered to Poland. The second digit denoted the year quarter of delivery; the third, the month of delivery; and the fourth, the last digit of the construction number.

As a curiosity, two or three Su-20s had cockpit stencilling in English. These were replaced during the first overhaul.

February 1976 saw the first crash, caused by engine failure in the Su-20 c/n 6601. mjr Jerzy Doliniec was killed. To replace the lost aircraft, in 1977 the maker supplied Su-20 c/n 74105 to Powidz. This was the 27th aircraft of the type that joined the Polish Air Force.

Notably, the first six Su-20s delivered to Poland in 1974 and the later machines with construction numbers ending with a '0' or '5' were factory fitted with AFA-39 (A-39) cameras. These machines were known as the Su-20R (R for 'razvedivatelniy', reconnaissance).

In 1977 KKR-1 reconnaissance pod were introduced in the Powidz-based unit. The pod housed, among other things, day and night cameras, a block of flash cartridges and an ELINT station. The reconnaissance pod could be carried by aircraft from the second shipment, from the 74th and 76th production batches. The first six machines had no such option as they were not fitted with appropriate wiring. For the same reason the KKR-1 pod could not be carried by '7125'.

[78-84]: Arming and pre-flight servicing of an Su-20. Photos 81 and 83 depict the KKR-1 reconnaissance pod.

85 | *Su-20 c/n 6602 '02', 7th Operational Reconnaissance Aviation Brigade (7 BLRO), Powidz.*

86

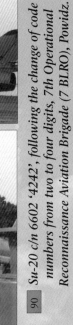

87

90 | *Su-20 c/n 6602 '4242', following the change of code numbers from two to four digits, 7th Operational Reconnaissance Aviation Brigade (7 BLRO), Powidz.*

88

[86-89]: *Su-20 c/n 6602 '4242'. The first Su-20s arrived in the 7th Operational Reconnaissance Aviation Brigade (7 BLRO) at Powidz on 26 April 1974. They were six machines of the 66th production batch (S-32MK). They had consecutive construction numbers 6601 to 6606, and code numbers '01' to '06'. In 1975 two-digit numbers on Su-20s were replaced with four-digit ones of '4241' to '4246'.*

89

Polish Wings

The Sukhoi Su-20s delivered to the Polish Air Force had a total useful life of 1, 800 hours of operation or 20 years. The first overhaul was due after 800 flying hours or 10 years. The next overhaul was carried out after 700 flying hours or 9 years. After the Il-28s were phased out in 1977, the 7 BLBR became a two-flight unit, operating the Su-20 and some Su-7U combat trainers since the Su-20 did not have a two-seat variant. Introduction of the Su-20 signified change in the brigade's duties, as the Su-20s were twin-role machines, able to strike enemy targets deep behind the lines and to perform effective photo and radio-electronic reconnaissance by day and night. The Su-20s were also potential carriers of tactical nuclear weapons.

The 7 BLBR, the sole operator of the type in Poland, was renamed again on 15 October 1982. By the decree of the Chief of the General Staff no. 024/ Org. of 4 May 1982 the unit was reformed into the 7th Bomber-Reconnaissance Aviation Regiment.

In December 1983 a group of young newly commissioned pilots arrived directly from the Air Force Officers Academy

[91]: Su-20 c/n 6603 '03'. All Su-20 aircraft delivered to Poland were silver, with red code numbers. Those numbers were applied using two styles of stencils.

[92]: Su-20 c/n 6603 '4243' Crashed near Powidz on 1 September 1987. Pilot mjr Andrzej Pawul ejected safely 7 seconds after take-off.

[93-95]: Su-20 c/n 6604 '4244'. Following the second overhaul by the Repair Works at Baranovichi the Su-20s were repainted in disruptive camouflage, intended to be the same as that used in the USSR at the time.

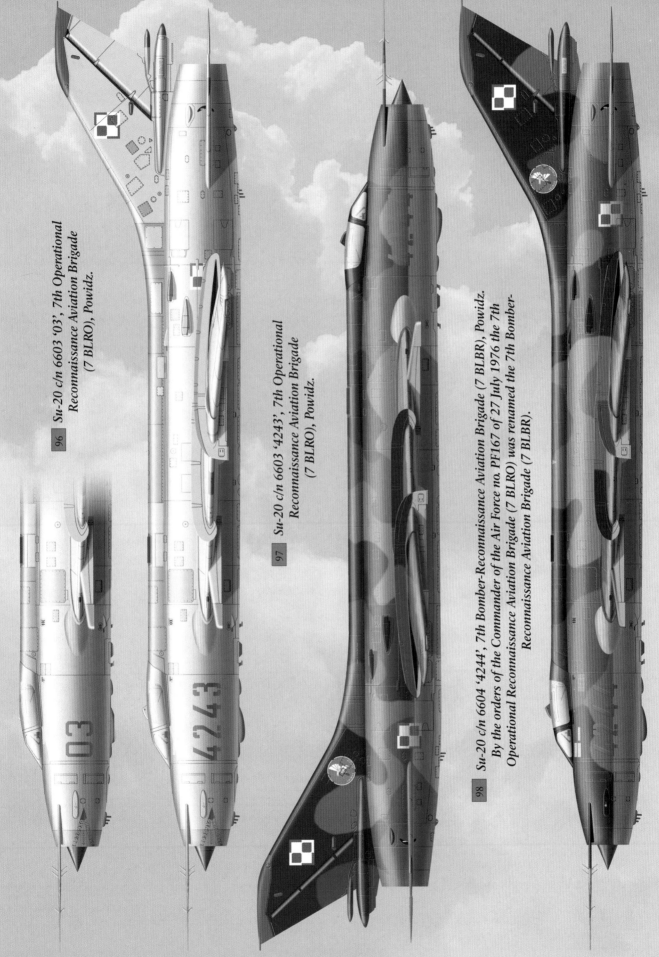

96 · *Su-20 c/n 6603 '03', 7th Operational Reconnaissance Aviation Brigade (7 BLRO), Powidz.*

97 · *Su-20 c/n 6603 '4243', 7th Operational Reconnaissance Aviation Brigade (7 BLRO), Powidz.*

98 · *Su-20 c/n 6604 '4244', 7th Bomber-Reconnaissance Aviation Brigade (7 BLBR), Powidz. By the orders of the Commander of the Air Force no. PF167 of 27 July 1976 the 7th Operational Reconnaissance Aviation Brigade (7 BLRO) was renamed the 7th Bomber-Reconnaissance Aviation Brigade (7 BLBR).*

[99, 100]: Su-20 c/n 6605 '05' delivered to Poland on 26 April 1974.

[101, 102]: Su-20 c/n 6605 '4245'. The same aircraft as in the photos above, in the disruptive camouflage it received following the second overhaul by the Repair Works at Baranovichi.

[103-105]: Su-20 c/n 6606 '06' delivered to Poland on 26 April 1974. Su-20 c/n 6606 '4246' in disruptive camouflage. The machine was scrapped in December 1995 at the Aircraft Depot at Mierzęcice. The aircraft had logged a total of 1, 256 hours 49 minutes flying time.

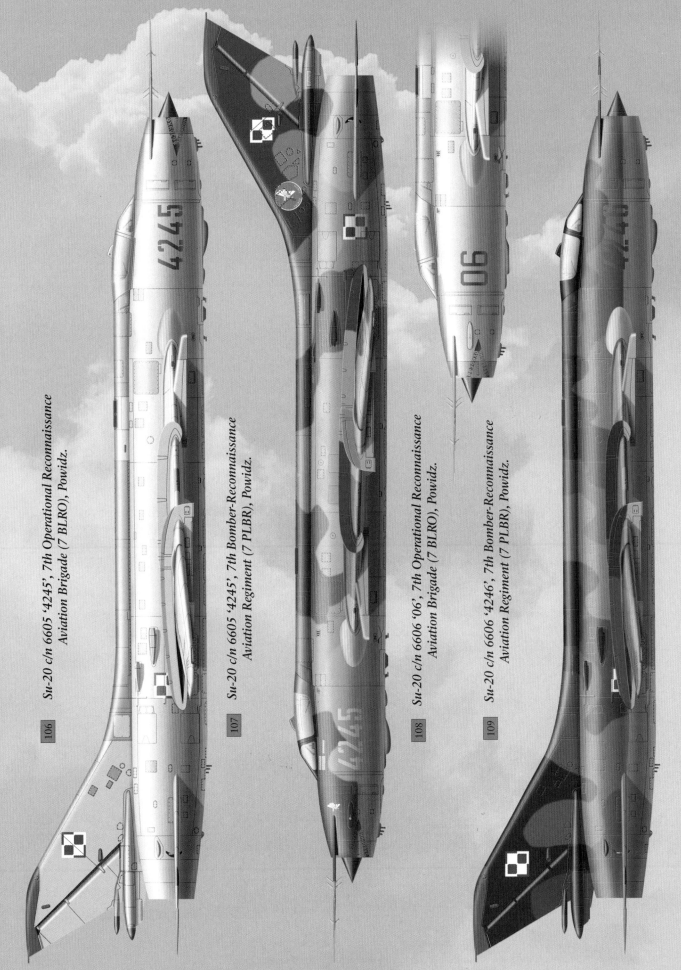

106   *Su-20 c/n 6605 '4245', 7th Operational Reconnaissance Aviation Brigade (7 BLRO), Powidz.*

107   *Su-20 c/n 6605 '4245', 7th Bomber-Reconnaissance Aviation Regiment (7 PLBR), Powidz.*

108   *Su-20 c/n 6606 '06', 7th Operational Reconnaissance Aviation Brigade (7 BLRO), Powidz.*

109   *Su-20 c/n 6606 '4246', 7th Bomber-Reconnaissance Aviation Regiment (7 PLBR), Powidz.*

[110, 111]: Su-20 c/n 74930 '6130', delivered to Poland in March 1976. The machine was destroyed in the Baltic Sea on 17 June 1988 following a collision with a bomb-target. The pilot kpt. Czesław Gibaszewski ejected safely.

[112, 113]: Su-20 c/n 74724 '6134'. The machine was lost on 31 May 1995 in a crash at Strzelin. kpt. Grzegorz Falenta was killed. The aircraft is in the disruptive camouflage it received following the second overhaul by the Repair Works at Baranovichi (in the then Byelorussian Soviet Republic).

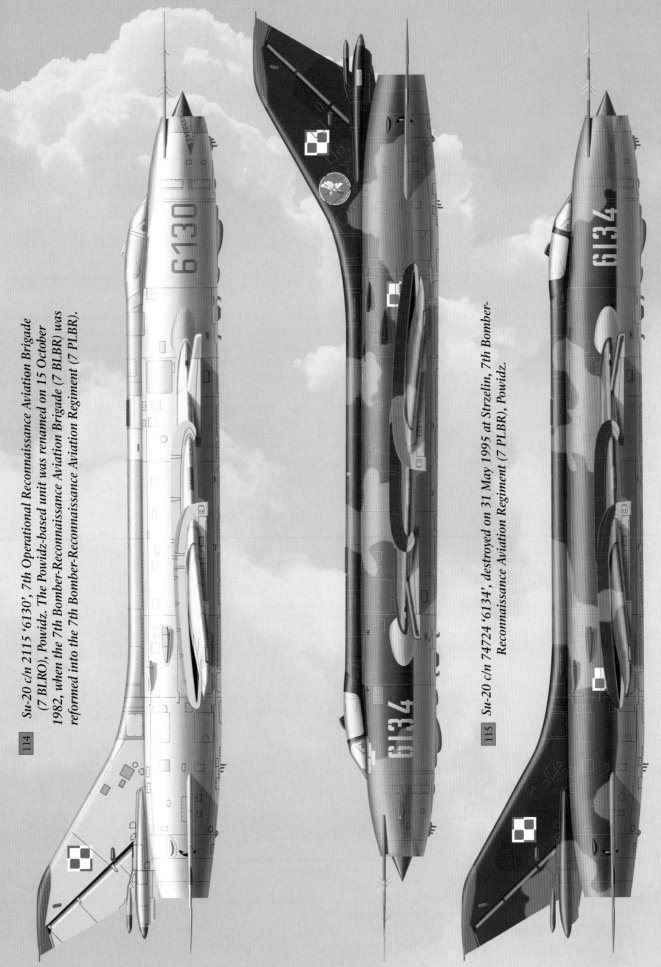

114 Su-20 c/n 2115 '6130', 7th Operational Reconnaissance Aviation Brigade (7 BLRO), Powidz. The Powidz-based unit was renamed on 15 October 1982, when the 7th Bomber-Reconnaissance Aviation Brigade (7 BLBR) was reformed into the 7th Bomber-Reconnaissance Aviation Regiment (7 PLBR).

115 Su-20 c/n 74724 '6134', destroyed on 31 May 1995 at Strzelin, 7th Bomber-Reconnaissance Aviation Regiment (7 PLBR), Powidz.

[116, 117]: *Su-20 c/n 74725 '6135', delivered to Poland in April 1976. In early 1992, during the second overhaul at Baranovichi the aircraft received disruptive camouflage.*

(WOSL) at Dęblin. Until then only pilots from combat units with substantial experience converted onto the Su-20.

At that time two pilots saved their Su-20 in difficult situations. On 17 May 1984 kpt. Andrzej Pawul hit a stork in mid-air. With his face injured by pieces of glass and his eyes 'stuck' with remains of the bird he managed nevertheless to land safely at Powidz. For this feat he was awarded the 'Distinguished Military Pilot' badge. Another incident took place on 4 September 1985. When firing an S-24 heavy unguided missile the engine

stalled, but kpt. Krzysztof Ryniecki managed to restart his engine at very low level and landed safely at his home base.

In the summer of 1987 one Su-20 flight visited the base of the Czechoslovak 6th Fighter-Bomber Aviation Regiment at Přerov. At the same time a flight of Czechoslovak MiG-21s from that regiment visited Powidz

In 1987 the Su-20-equipped 7 PLBR became part of the Piła-based 2nd Fighter-Bomber Aviation Division (along with the 6 PLMB - Piła and 45 LPSzB - Babimost), after several years when it reported directly to the Air Force HQ.

[118-120]: *On 28 February 1997 the aircraft was delivered to the repair works in Bydgoszcz by kpt. pil. Donat Kluj. On that occasion ground crews adorned the machine with chalked messages.*

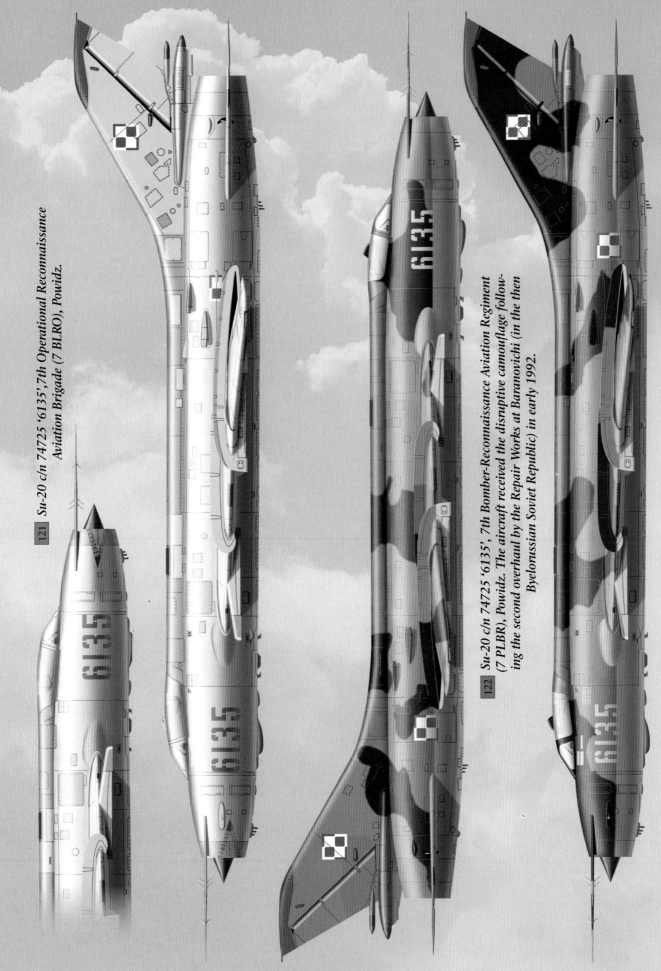

121 *Su-20 c/n 74725 '6135', 7th Operational Reconnaissance Aviation Brigade (7 BLRO), Powidz.*

122 *Su-20 c/n 74725 '6135', 7th Bomber-Reconnaissance Aviation Regiment (7 PLBR), Powidz. The aircraft received the disruptive camouflage following the second overhaul by the Repair Works at Baranovichi (in the then Byelorussian Soviet Republic) in early 1992.*

[123-126]: Su-20 c/n 74726 '6136', delivered to Poland in March 1976.

123

124

125

126

[127-130]: KKR-1 reconnaissance pod can be seen on the under-fuselage hardpoint. The pod housed day and night cameras, a block of flash cartridges and an ELINT station. The reconnaissance pod could be carried by aircraft from the second shipment, from 74th and 76th production batches. Following the second overhaul by the Repair Works at Baranovichi the aircraft were repainted in disruptive camouflage. Code numbers were re-applied in yellow. No. '7125' was an exception (red numbers). The aircraft shown in these photos ('6136') also had yellow numbers initially (photo above), but these were subsequently repainted white with red outline. This was done by the aircraft's ground crew chief st. sierż. sztab. Wojciech 'Bomba' Krygowski.

127

128

129

130

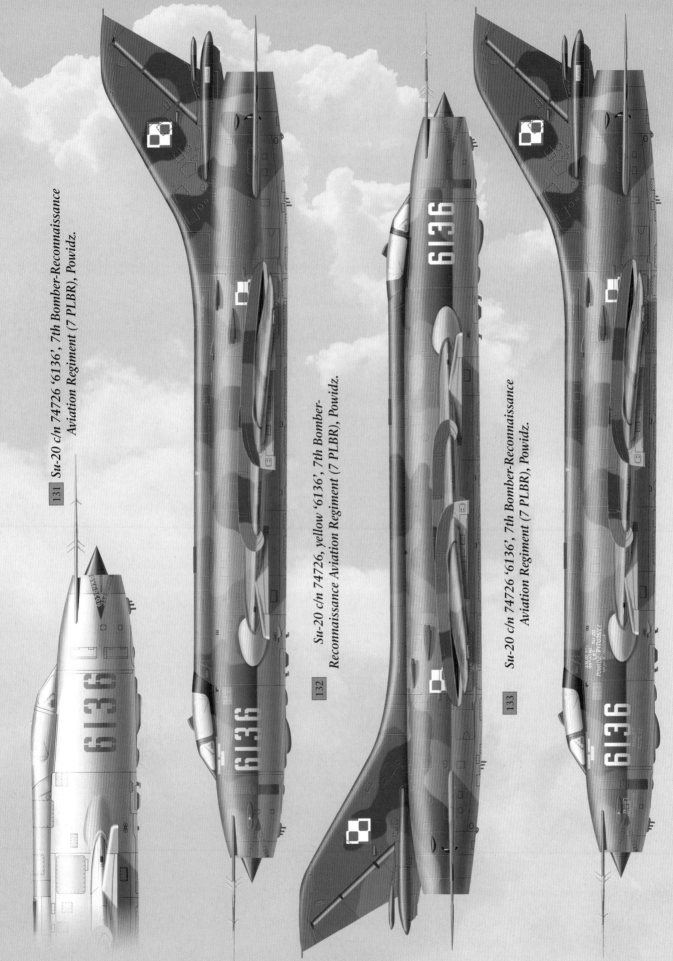

131 *Su-20 c/n 74726 '6136', 7th Bomber-Reconnaissance Aviation Regiment (7 PLBR), Powidz.*

132 *Su-20 c/n 74726, yellow '6136', 7th Bomber-Reconnaissance Aviation Regiment (7 PLBR), Powidz.*

133 *Su-20 c/n 74726 '6136', 7th Bomber-Reconnaissance Aviation Regiment (7 PLBR), Powidz.*

[134]: *Flypast of Su-20 formation over Powidz aerodrome on 28 February 1997. The aircraft were ferried away to the WZL-2 in Bydgoszcz.*

[135]: *Su-20 c/n 74727 '6137', delivered to Poland in March 1976.*

[136]: *On 13 March 1077 the aircraft, flown by mjr Stanisław Walczak was damaged during landing. The pilot touched down too far down the runway, overshot, and the aircraft overturned.*

[137]: *Su-20 c/n 74728 '6138', delivered to Poland in March 1976. The KKR-1 reconnaissance pod can be seen on the under-fuselage hardpoint. These pods could be carried only by machines of the 74th and 76th production batch. These aircraft were often referred to as the Su-20R (reconnaissance).*

138   *Su-20 c/n 74727 '6137', 7th Bomber-Reconnaissance Aviation Regiment (7 PLBR), Powidz.*

139   *Su-20 c/n 74828 '6138', 7th Bomber-Reconnaissance Aviation Regiment (7 PLBR), Powidz.*

During the last years of its existence the 7 PLBR had very good training results. It became a showcase unit of the Polish Air Force and was visited by numerous western delegations. The first such visit took place on 16 October 1990, when the regiment was visited by several dozen officers of the Royal Swedish Air Force. This was the first occasion when it demonstrated the 'strike evasion' (a nearly simultaneous take-off of over a dozen aircraft from all available runway surfaces, including several aircraft taking off from opposite ends of the main runway with minimum time interval).

Following nearly twenty years of Su-20 operations by the Polish Air Force the aircraft started to gradually wear out. By mid-1990s they only equipped a single flight of the regiment, the other flight using the Su-22. The end of Su-20 operations came in February 1997. On 25 and 26 February the last ten serviceable aircraft moved to Bydgoszcz. They were '6136', '6138', '6256', '6264', '6265' (to Bydgoszcz on 25 February), and '6135', '6250', '6252', '6259' and '6262' (26 February 1997)

Following several months of storage the aircraft started to be broken up, ending the Su-20 history in Poland. Several Su-20s from Powidz went to public and private collections.

[140, 141]: *Su-20 c/n 74210 '6250', delivered to Poland in April 1976. The aircraft made its last flight on 28 February 1997, when kpt. A Paczkowski ferried it to the WZL-2 in Bydgoszcz.*

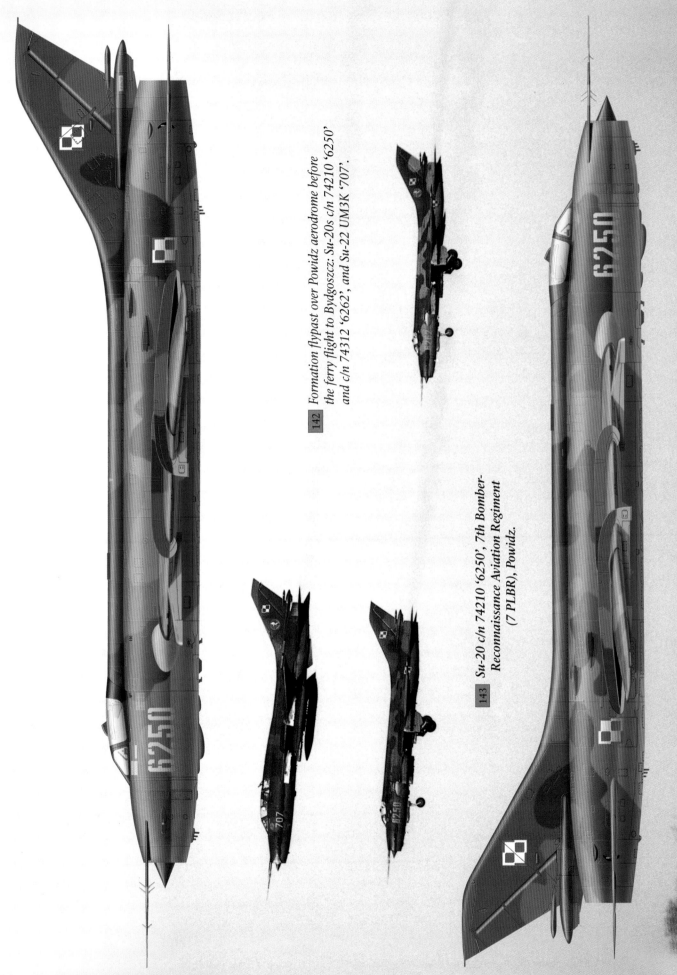

142 *Formation flypast over Powidz aerodrome before the ferry flight to Bydgoszcz: Su-20s c/n 74210 '6250' and c/n 74312 '6262', and Su-22 UM3K '707'.*

143 *Su-20 c/n 74210 '6250', 7th Bomber-Reconnaissance Aviation Regiment (7 PLBR), Powidz.*

[144-151]: *Su-20 c/n 76302 '6252', delivered to Poland in April 1976. The aircraft received the disruptive camouflage following the second overhaul by the Repair Works at Baranovichi, and continued to fly in it until 28 February 1997 when kpt. Grzegorz Pawłowski made its last flight, delivering it to the WZL-2 in Bydgoszcz. The aircraft logged a total flying time of 1, 324 hrs 4 mins.*

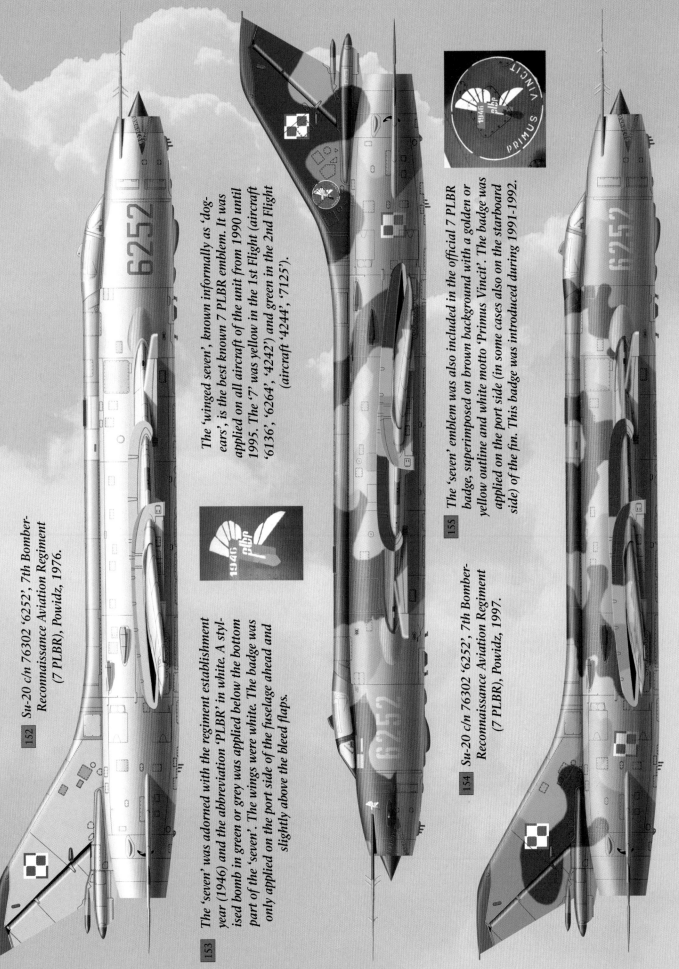

152 Su-20 c/n 76302 '6252', 7th Bomber-Reconnaissance Aviation Regiment (7 PLBR), Powidz, 1976.

153 The 'seven' was adorned with the regiment establishment year (1946) and the abbreviation 'PLBR' in white. A stylised bomb in green or grey was applied below the bottom part of the 'seven'. The wings were white. The badge was only applied on the port side of the fuselage ahead and slightly above the bleed flaps.

The 'winged seven', known informally as 'dog-ears', is the best known 7 PLBR emblem. It was applied on all aircraft of the unit from 1990 until 1995. The '7' was yellow in the 1st Flight (aircraft '6136', '6264', '4242') and green in the 2nd Flight (aircraft '4244', '7125').

155 The 'seven' emblem was also included in the official 7 PLBR badge, superimposed on brown background with a golden or yellow outline and white motto 'Primus Vincit'. The badge was applied on the port side (in some cases also on the starboard side) of the fin. This badge was introduced during 1991-1992.

154 Su-20 c/n 76302 '6252', 7th Bomber-Reconnaissance Aviation Regiment (7 PLBR), Powidz, 1997.

C/N	CODE NO.	SERVICE PERIOD		NOTES
		FROM	TO	
6601	01	04.1974	03.02.1976	Crashed at Kazimierz Biskupi. Kpt. Jerzy Doliniec killed.
6602	02 / 4242	04.1974	28.02.1994	Currently on display at the MLP in Cracow.
6603	03 / 4243	04.1974	01.09.1987	Destroyed near Powidz. Mjr Andrzej Pawul ejected safely 7 seconds after take-off.
6604	04 / 4244	04.1974	28.02.1994	Scrapped
6605	05 / 4245	04.1974	28.02.1994	Since 1996 on display at the Poznań Citadel Museum.
6606	06 / 4246	04.1974	28.02.1994	Scrapped on 7 December 1995.
74930	6130	03.1976	17.06.1988	Destroyed in the Baltic Sea on 13 June 1988 following a collision with a bomb-target. Kpt. Czesław Gibaszewski ejected safely.
76301	6131	03.1976	06.04.1994	Currently on display at the MWP in Warsaw.
74724	6134	03.1976	31.05.1995	Crashed at Strzelin. Kpt. Grzegorz Falenta killed.
74725	6135	03.1976	28.02.1997	Delivered by air to WZL-2 in Bydgoszcz.
74726	6136	03.1976	28.02.1997	Delivered by air to WZL-2 in Bydgoszcz.
74727	6137	03.1976	13.03.1977	Following accident transferred to **COSSTWL** at Oleśnica.
74828	6138	03.1976	28.02.1997	Delivered by air to WZL-2 in Bydgoszcz. Currently on display at the Lubuskie Muzeum Wojskowe, Drzonów
74829	6139	03.1976	18.08.1980	Crashed at Solec Kujawski. Kpt. Ryszard Pawłowicz ejected safely.
74210	6250	04.1976	28.02.1997	Delivered by air to WZL-2 in Bydgoszcz.
74311	6251	04.1976	01.08.1990	Crashed at Nadarzyce firing range. Por. Jerzy Gruszczyński ejected safely.
76302	6252	04.1976	28.02.1997	Delivered by air to WZL-2 in Bydgoszcz.
76303	6253	04.1976	25.06.1992	Currently on display at Powidz Air Base.
76304	6254	04.1976	14.07.1993	Crashed at Września. Por. Robert Dudzic ejected safely.
76305	6255	04.1976	1994	Currently on display at a private collection at Łódź-Lublinek aerodrome.
74416	6256	04.1976	28.02.1997	Delivered by air to WZL-2 in Bydgoszcz. Currently on display in Broniszew near Białobrzegi (south of Warsaw)
74209	6259	04.1976	28.02.1997	Delivered by air to WZL-2 in Bydgoszcz.
74312	6262	04.1976	28.02.1997	Delivered by air to WZL-2 in Bydgoszcz. (Display in Tarnów ??)
74313	6263	04.1976	22.05.1978	Crashed at Bednary. Por. Antoni Dziadowiec killed.
74314	6264	04.1976	28.02.1997	Delivered by air to WZL-2 in Bydgoszcz.
74415	6265	04.1976	28.02.1997	Delivered by air to WZL-2 in Bydgoszcz. Currently on display at the Air Force Officers Academy (WSOSP) at Dęblin.
74105	7125	02.1977	19.08.1996	Delivered by air for the Air Show in Bydgoszcz. Did not return to the unit.

[156,157, 159]: Su-20 c/n 76303 '6253', delivered to Poland in April 1976. The machine, along with nos. '6131' and '6255' remained silver throughout their service, because they did not undergo the second major overhaul due to disintegration of the USSR. It is currently on display at Powidz Air Base.

156

158 The 'winged seven', known informally as 'dog-ears', is the best known 7 PLBR emblem. It was applied on all aircraft of the unit from 1990 until 1995. The '7' was yellow in the 1st Flight (aircraft '6136', '6264', '4242') and green in the 2nd Flight (aircraft '4244', '7125').

160 Su-20 c/n 76303 '6253', 7th Bomber-Reconnaissance Aviation Regiment (7 PLBR), Powidz.

163

7 PLBR badge as used during 1980s.

[161, 162, 164]: Su-20 c/n 74416 '6256', 7th Bomber-Reconnaissance Aviation Regiment (7 PLBR), Powidz, 1997.

161

162

164

165　*Su-20 c/n 74416 '6256', 7th Bomber-Reconnaissance Aviation Regiment (7 PLBR), Powidz.*

166　*Su-20 c/n 74416 '6256', 7th Bomber-Reconnaissance Aviation Regiment (7 PLBR), Powidz, 1997.*

[167, 168]: Su-20 c/n 74416 '6256', delivered to Poland in April 1976. The aircraft made its last flight on 28 February 1997, when kpt. Grzegorz Pawłowski delivered it to the WZL-2 in Bydgoszcz. The aircraft is currently on display at a petrol station at Broniszew near Białobrzegi, south of Warsaw.

COLOURS OF THE SU-20

All Su-20 aircraft delivered to Poland were silver (FS 17178), with red code numbers. Those numbers were applied using two styles of stencils. Following the second overhaul by the Repair Works at Baranovichi the aircraft were repainted in disruptive camouflage, intended to be the same as that used in the USSR at the time. Code numbers were re-applied in yellow. The only exceptions were aircraft '6136' (white no.) and '7125' (red). Aircraft '6131', '6253' and '6255' remained silver throughout their service, because they did not undergo the second major overhaul due to disintegration of the USSR.

Comparison of individual Su-20s reveals great variety in camouflage schemes. Their colours and general layout were similar. Despite the differences in colour arrangement, three colour schemes could be identified on the Su-20s, composed of the following colours (see table on the right).

Undercarriage and wheel wells were initially painted light grey FS 36293, then grey FS 36495. Wheel discs were green FS 34 138. Aerials and aerial fairings were green FS 14090. No general scheme can be given for Polish Air Force Su-20s. Colours and shapes of individual areas were different on different aircraft, so the Su-20 schemes have to be analysed individually for each aircraft.

I	
Olive green	FS 34 082
Sand	FS 30 450
Grey green	FS 36 360
Green	FS 34 151
Pale blue	FS 35 190
II	
Olive Green	FS 34 096
Brown	FS 30 061
Sand	FS 30 450
Pale Blue	FS 14 090
Green	FS 24 110
Blue grey	FS 35 414
III	
Olive Green	FS 34 096
Brown	FS 30 061
Sand	FS 30 450
Pale Blue	FS 14 090
Tan	FS 30 219
Light olive	FS 32 108
Pale green	FS 24 138
Blue grey	FS 35 414

[169]: Su-20R. The KKR-1 reconnaissance pod can be seen on the under-fuselage hardpoint. On the port side of the fin note the 7 PLBR badge with the motto 'Primus Vincit' ('The first one wins').

169

[170-172]: Su-20 c/n 74209 '6259', delivered to Poland in April 1976. The aircraft made its last flight on 28 February 1997, when kpt. Grzegorz Pawłowski delivered it to the WZL-2 in Bydgoszcz. The aircraft logged a total flying time of 1, 342 hrs 20 mins.

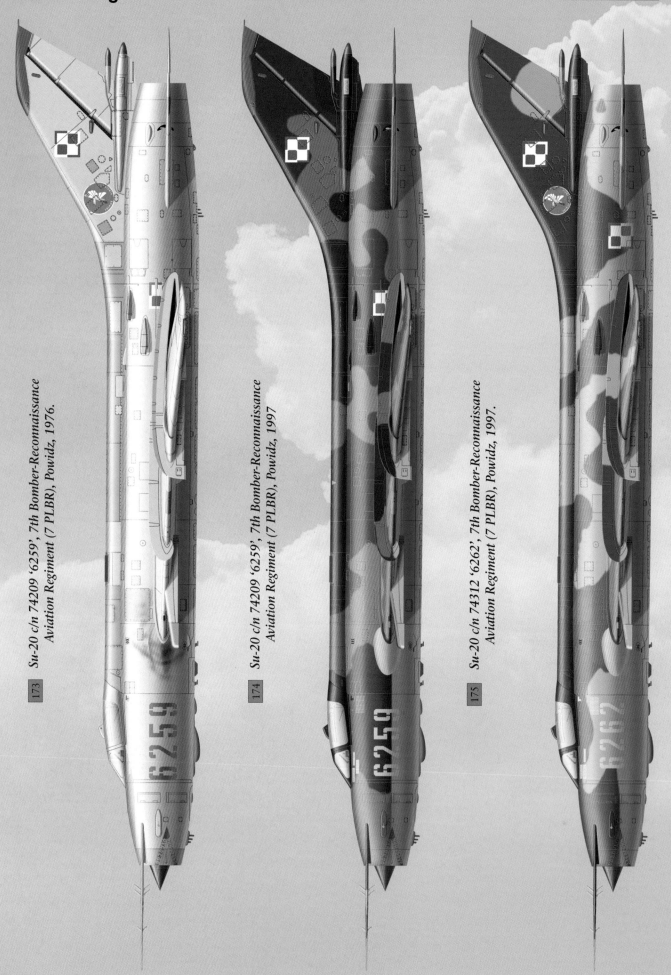

173 *Su-20 c/n 74209 '6259', 7th Bomber-Reconnaissance Aviation Regiment (7 PLBR), Powidz, 1976.*

174 *Su-20 c/n 74209 '6259', 7th Bomber-Reconnaissance Aviation Regiment (7 PLBR), Powidz, 1997*

175 *Su-20 c/n 74312 '6262', 7th Bomber-Reconnaissance Aviation Regiment (7 PLBR), Powidz, 1997.*

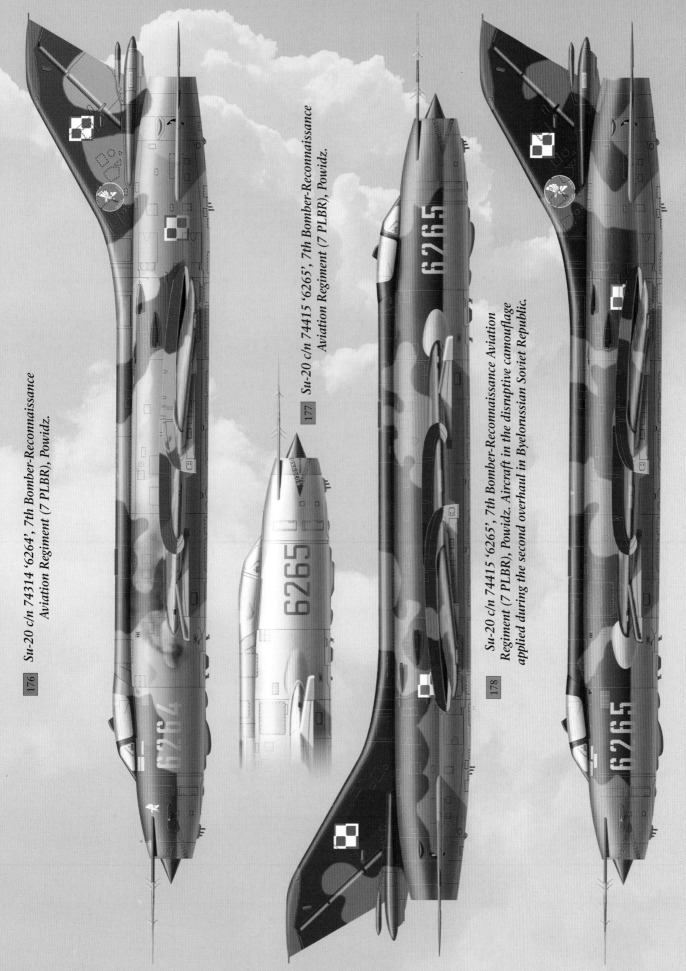

176 *Su-20 c/n 74314 '6264', 7th Bomber-Reconnaissance Aviation Regiment (7 PLBR), Powidz.*

177 *Su-20 c/n 74415 '6265', 7th Bomber-Reconnaissance Aviation Regiment (7 PLBR), Powidz.*

178 *Su-20 c/n 74415 '6265', 7th Bomber-Reconnaissance Aviation Regiment (7 PLBR), Powidz. Aircraft in the disruptive camouflage applied during the second overhaul in Byelorussian Soviet Republic.*

[179]: Su-20 c/n 74314 '6264' and c/n 74415 '6265', 7 PLBR, Powidz.

[180-182, 185]: Su-20 c/n 74415 '6265', delivered to Poland in April 1976. The machine displays the badge of the Powidz-based 7 PLBR on the fin. The aircraft is currently on display at the Air Force Officers Academy (WSOSP) at Dęblin.

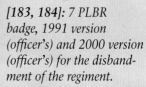

[183, 184]: 7 PLBR badge, 1991 version (officer's) and 2000 version (officer's) for the disbandment of the regiment.

56